I0785320

Argument Structure

Secrets of the World's Best Debaters –
Master the Structure of Arguments

Contents

INTRODUCTION 1

CHAPTER 1: START STRONG 2

CHAPTER 2: ORGANIZING YOUR IDEAS 7

CHAPTER 3: COMPELLING CONCLUSIONS 16

CHAPTER 4: WATCH YOUR LANGUAGE! 22

CHAPTER 5: MASTERING THE ART OF ANALOGY 26

CHAPTER 6: BURDEN OF PROOF – CONVINCE THEM YOU'RE
RIGHT 30

CHAPTER 7: THE ART OF DEDUCTION (AND INDUCTION) 40

CHAPTER 8: SOPHISTRY! IDENTIFYING LOGICAL FALLACIES 44

CHAPTER 9: ORAL ARGUMENTS 53

CHAPTER 10: WRITING AN ARGUMENTATIVE ESSAY 57

CONCLUSION 64

Introduction

Argumentation isn't just about being the loudest or most right; it is about self-presentation and the art of logic. Whether you are in competitive speech and debate, looking for a way to defend your beliefs, or just getting ready for the infamous Thanksgiving Dinner with Uncle Joe, this book will help you become a master of argumentation.

The following chapters will discuss how to structure your argument from premise to conclusion. You will learn how to choose examples and analogies, how to back up your claims with authorities on your subject, and how to use and interpret data to help you make your case. We will see how to identify and avoid logical fallacies and finish off with two chapters on oral and written arguments.

There are plenty of books on this subject on the market, so thank you for choosing this one! Every effort was made to ensure it is full of as much useful information as possible.

Enjoy!

Chapter 1: Start Strong

The hardest part of starting anything is figuring out where best to begin. We might possess some vague idea that an argument should begin with a premise, but how do we select the premises, and how do we establish them without beginning another argument?

Premises

Premises form the foundation of each part of your argument, so you want them to be both clear and simple. The truth of the premise will justify your following arguments, so you also want them to be self-evident – or at least something that you *and* your opponent will not dispute. It is important to remember: you cannot ever win an argument where you and your opponent do not agree upon certain premises. So how do we find the premise of our argument?

Chances are, you already know the conclusion of your argument, or else you probably would not be arguing in the first place. The conclusion is whatever you want to get or prove. Perhaps you want your boss to give you a raise, or you want to prove to a friend that a particular political candidate is immoral or destructive. Because we know our conclusion so well, and because we are passionate about it, we often make the mistake of starting with the conclusion and trying to work backward.

While this gives us an easy beginning, and might even start an animated conversation, it is not likely to convince your opponent, because all they have to do is contradict you with their own conclusion. Remember, they are as passionate about their ideas as you are about yours, and they will not give them up easily. If you start contradicting each other immediately, the conversation will turn into a quarrel that is not much more sophisticated than a continuous repetition of "Is not!" "Is too!"

The scientist Blaise Pascal gave two rules for axioms (which are a kind of premise) in his essay, "The Art of Persuasion":

1. Not to omit any necessary principle without asking whether it is admitted, however clear and evident it may be.
2. Not to demand, in axioms, any but things that are perfectly evident of themselves.

In modern English, we might say we ought not to assume that something does not need to be proved. This is not an exercise in skepticism, but a search for foundational points upon which you and your opponent agree. You and your boss might not agree that you ought to get a raise, but they might agree with you that you work hard. If they don't agree that you work hard, they might agree that you work overtime, or that you have done well on several recent projects. If your boss accepts that you are a hard worker, you put them in the awkward position of either giving you the raise you want or trying to argue why a good employee who works hard shouldn't get a raise.

To find your premise, take your knowledge of what you want to prove and think backward. What is something foundational to your conclusion that both you and your opponent believe? Words like *for*, *since*, and *because* will indicate to you that you might have found a premise. One simple example can be found in this classic truism:

All men are mortal. Socrates is a man. Therefore, Socrates is mortal.

This statement has two premises:

1. All men are mortal
2. Socrates is a man.

If we admit that all men are mortal and that Socrates is a man, then we must logically conclude that Socrates is mortal.

Let's say you want to argue that the death penalty should be abolished because many people are sentenced to death because of mistakes and careless work by police and prosecutors, not because they are guilty. This statement has one premise:

1. Many people are sentenced to death because of mistakes and careless work by police and prosecutors.

If you and your opponent agree that the police and the prosecutors are often careless and fatally fallible, then you can continue your debate over whether or not this carelessness fallibility justifies eliminating the death penalty. If they don't think that the police or prosecutors are careless, your argument will not mean anything to them because they do not accept the premise of it.

If this happens you might need to start further back, with simpler premises:

Premise: Many people have been cleared of all charges *after* their execution

Conclusion: Prosecutors and police are careless or fallible.

For an extended argument (which we will look at in depth later) a conclusion will become the premise for the next step.

Premise: Prosecutors and police are careless or fallible

Conclusion: The death penalty ought to be abolished.

If you are still having a little trouble identifying premises for yourself, that is okay. We will see lots more as we continue learning how to structure our arguments.

Definitions

Another important element of beginning an argument is defining your terms. This prevents confusion and getting sidetracked over arguing about the meaning of a word. It can also sometimes undermine your opponent's arguments.

Some words mean different things to different people, so it can be essential to clarify anything that might be ambiguous. It might even end debate altogether: I have often come up short in the midst of heated arguments upon realizing that my opponent and I agreed! We were just using different words that the other one didn't understand in the way we did.

So, what terms should you define and how should you define them?

1. Terms which are obscure. If you use technical language, make sure everyone knows what you mean. The same with unfamiliar words or words which could have two meanings.

You inevitably use technical language in whatever fields you master. If you engage in a particularly complex argument about science, history, or philosophy, you may spend a great deal of time immersed in books and lectures from experts in those fields. Each of these disciplines developed precise language to talk about their fields. It is your job to make sure that you interpret that language if your opponent – or those listening to you – does not understand it. Otherwise, your argument will be meaningless to them.

Be careful with words that can have two meanings, such as 'decimated'. In colloquial language, decimated means the same thing as destroy. Precisely defined, however, it means 'to reduce by 10%'. Other examples of words with two or more meanings include *pound*, *mean*, and *seal*. Be clear about which definition you intend to use.

2. Terms which are important to your argument.

Have you ever responded to a question such as, "Are you doing well?" with "It depends on what you mean by 'well'?" If so, then you have already used this technique.

Defining important terms will add immense clarity to your arguments and prevent you from getting trapped in your own words. If you were, for instance, to make the argument that "Alchemy is not science", it would be imperative to define what you meant by *science*. Otherwise, you might find your opponent countering that alchemists make hypotheses, do experiments, and record their results precisely – and therefore must be scientists. You will have to backpedal to your definition instead of starting with it and, in doing so, you will lose the thread of the argument.

Defining your terms early gives you the advantage of clarity. It prevents you from arguing pointlessly and gives your opponent the opportunity to propose alternate definitions which you may need to counter to prove your point.

Once you choose definitions, keep them and use them consistently. Even if you don't need to define a word to clarify your argument, use the same terms for the same ideas and objects throughout. One example is the way I use the word *argument* in this book. We are talking about *argument* as the method of using a progression of logic to prove a conclusion. Someone could hear *argument*, however, and think of a shouting match or other verbal altercation. So, when saying I want to teach you how to argue, I ought to be clear that I don't want to teach you how to win a shouting match or show you how to intimidate or beat down your opponent verbally. I want to teach you how to contend for your point clearly, calmly, and in a way that invites other people to see your position and agree with it.

We define *argument* as making a logical progression of ideas from premise to conclusion in a convincing way. If I switched on you mid-book – perhaps when we talk about what language to use – and started telling you not to argue with people, you would be justifiably confused.

To recap, remember: the thing you want to prove is your conclusion. Don't begin your argument with your conclusion; begin with the premise: the basic foundations of why you believe in your conclusion. As you build your premises, the words you need to define will often present themselves naturally. Make sure that you are clear and consistent in your language and that you, your opponent, and anyone listening, understands how any technical terminology is going to be used.

Chapter 2: Organizing Your Ideas

Now that you have your premise, you can set up a proof for your conclusions. Proofs provide the meat of your argument, so it is important for you to structure them in a way that everyone can follow without taking leaps in your reasoning.

Our premises gave us some sort of common ground with our opponent – now you want to show how and why you think about things in a different way. This requires a logical progression; never assume that your conclusion is self-evident given the premises.

Necessary Facts & Premises

Provide any relevant facts essential to your argument. These facts should be indisputable – or at least not topics that need to be disputed for the purpose of your argument. Think about this like a lawyer looking at evidence from a crime scene. Your facts should serve two purposes: to give context and to provide support for your position once you have interpreted them. (We will talk more about the interpretation of facts later).

However, just because these are facts does not mean they ought to be boring. Tell a story that a reader or listener can engage with. Part of giving your statement of fact is knowing your audience. What do they already know about the context of your argument? What do they care about?

Let's say I wanted to apply for a private grant because my scientific expedition to Antarctica was running out of money. I should check and find out whether or not the foundation is already funding Antarctic exploration and research.

If they are not, I ought to assume that they do not know anything at all about doing research near the South Pole, and spend a little time filling them in.

Premise: It is valuable to fund scientific expeditions and research.

I believe this because I am a scientist and need money. They believe this because their foundation is known to give scientists money. So, we have some common beliefs to start from.

Statement of Fact: I am Jane Smith, PhD, and I have been studying penguins in Antarctica with my team since 2015. Now we are out of money and will have to go home if we cannot raise more funds, but we have not finished our research.

As you have probably noticed, that statement of fact contains all the relevant information, but it is not very interesting. Now, I do not want to spend too much time just stating facts, but I want to give my audience enough information that they know why they should care about the argument I am about to present:

My team and I arrived in Antarctica in July 2015 with a mission to study the local penguin colony. For the last three years, we have followed them on their journeys to their mating grounds, watched them raise their chicks, and saw those chicks mature and find their own mates. We have been given an unprecedented opportunity to study a colony over an extended period of time, and we hoped to be here at least one year longer. Unfortunately, due to unexpected repairs required by some of our equipment after the last blizzard, we may have to cut short our mission if we cannot raise further funding.

Although this statement of fact takes a much more sympathetic spin, I have not said anything that needs to be proved (in this hypothetical scenario). Now, my audience has the necessary information they need to understand my following argument – 12 Reasons Why My Penguin Research Expedition Should Get Your Grant – and I have invited them to care.

It is important to back up your statement of fact with the proper research for the topic. Sometimes you are the expert in the situation, as Jane Smith, PhD, is an expert in the financial situation of her team. At other times, you may need to cite historical authorities or scientific studies. We'll talk more about how to choose those later. For now, remember that your statement of fact should be indisputable and engaging.

Logical Progression of Ideas

This is where you will lay out the reasons for your conclusion. Depending on the complexity of your argument, you may move quickly from the premise to conclusion, or you may need to offer several proofs. If the conclusion does not follow immediately from the premises, you will need to take the time to fill in the gaps.

Each paragraph or thought ought to follow a clear structure: the idea you want to discuss, the evidence for your argument, and a demonstration of the significance of that evidence. Start with the idea you want to prove, offered as a proposition, not something already concluded: "It's no good shutting the barn door after the horses are gone." Next, give evidence relevant to that proposition: "The horses are no longer in the barn." This may be facts or data, information from studies, or just your own observations, depending on the nature of the argument. End by showing why this evidence supports your proposition: "Because the horses are currently outside the barn, shutting the door will not keep them inside."

Writers and debaters use several different methods of progression to provide a structure for their ideas. They usually fall under *Time Order*, *Order of Importance*, and *Order of Specificity*.

Time Order works best when presenting a sequence of connected events or steps in a process. "First A happened, then B happened, then C happened." Historians use this when arguing for the reasons that a commander lost a battle or a king lost his throne. For instance, if I wanted to prove that the French Revolution happened because the people were starving, I might proceed something like this:

1. In the late 18th Century, most grain produced by French farmers was exported, rather than remaining with the people.
2. Because they did not have enough grain, the people became hungry. Famine and grain riots caused social unrest.
3. Because there were riots, the government had to pursue some kind of political reform to restore order.
4. To restore order, King Louis XVI called the Estates General in 1789.
5. The Estates General deadlocked and was unable to present a resolution to the problems that started the riots.
6. The people revolted, beginning with the storming of the Bastille on July 14, 1789.

Using this progression of events over time, I can provide a compelling argument that famine provided the catalyst for the French Revolution.

Be careful when using time order to provide a proof, since A is not necessarily the cause of B just because it happened before it: i.e. "Jim came into the kitchen, and then the stove caught on fire. Therefore, the stove caught on fire because Jim came into the kitchen." The sequence of events should be clearly connected to one another.

Order of Importance allows you to rank a sequence of ideas or proofs. Rhetorically speaking, it is most effective to begin with the least important and move up in seriousness or open with the arguments that support your idea the best.

Moving up in importance:

These windows should have curtains. Curtains are aesthetically pleasing. Curtains can dress up a room and don't cost very much, especially secondhand. Furthermore, our nosey neighbors are gawking at us all hours of the day and night, and curtains would block their view.

Moving down in importance:

We should outlaw the hunting of the burrowing owl; otherwise, it will go entirely extinct. These owls are a critical part of their native habitat. Bird-watchers like to look at burrowing owls. Furthermore, burrowing owls are extremely cute.

Moving up in importance allows you to build tension and end with a slam dunk. Moving down in importance catches your audience's attention quickly and can allow you to place weaker information later in the argument when people are paying less attention.

Order of Specificity is used to move between general and specific. Decide whether you want to begin with small details and expand to big ideas, or to begin with big ideas before focusing on detail. A big idea would be an ethical standard or general rule, while details would be particular cases. Building up and focusing on both have their merits, and you can choose between them based on your personal style and preferences. The thing to remember when using spatial order is not to jump back and forth between large and small. Either start small and get bigger or start big and become small. We will see more or specificity when we talk about deductive and inductive reasoning.

All these methods apply to both the construction of an element of a proof and the construction of the entire argument. Every larger argument is made up of a series of short ones, often with the conclusion of the last part forming the premises and assumptions of the next. This building block method will keep your logic watertight.

Here is an outline of a longer argument so you can see how the progression might look:

Thing to be proved: Texting while driving should be banned because it is as dangerous as driving drunk.

Premise: Driving while impaired is dangerous to the driver and everyone else in their vicinity.

Present the conclusion as a thing to be proved: If texting while driving produces similar effects as drunk driving, we should treat it in a similar way.

Step One: Provide a presentation of facts about accidents and fatalities caused by drunk driving. Clearly, this is dangerous. Bring up the laws against drunk driving.

A helpful way to figure out what ought to come next is to ask yourself the question, "So what?" or "What does that have to do with anything?"

Step Two: Provide a similar presentation of facts about accidents and fatalities caused by texting while driving. Bring up that it has not been treated the same way as drunk driving, even though it also is dangerous.

So what?

Step Three: Cite studies about the effects of phone multitasking on the focus of a driver and compare these effects to the effects of alcohol. Put a strong highlight on the similarities.

This process may take several paragraphs, depending on the detail you want to use for your argument. As you move from each paragraph to the next, you will want to provide a smooth transition. An essay or argument can stand alone, but a piece of that argument should be connected to the ideas before it and the ideas that will come after it.

Transitions take lots of practice, but if you keep in mind that you want to connect all the parts of your argument into one cohesive whole, and always look for the next logical step in the progression of your ideas, the transitions should present themselves. Don't leave people hanging and wondering why you came to a particular conclusion. Don't leave them wondering why you threw out a piece of information, either. An argument is not a place for random trivia. Everything should have a purpose.

Organization When Your Argument Is a Response

The way you organize ideas changes depending on if you are building your own idea, or directly responding to someone else. The easiest and most effective way to organize a response or refutation is to follow the sequence of your opponent's argument.

As an example, I will use a basic outline of a debate that took place in the Senate during January of 1830, between Daniel Webster, the Senator from Massachusetts, and Robert Hayne, the Senator from South Carolina. The Senate at this time is discussing who should have power over the sale of public lands in the west to new settlers: the states, or the federal government?

Haynes:

1. The federal government sells land to settlers at high prices.
2. The government that sells land at a high price plants a settlement which is immediately in debt and the settlement does not prosper. The inhabitants are exploited for capital nearly into poverty and almost into oblivion, the way England did to Ireland (read: not only bad but arguably immoral).
3. If the federal government uses these public lands for tax revenue, it will feed carelessness, corruption, and exploitation of the states at the federal level.
4. The responsibility for sale of public land should be given to the states so that the federal government cannot use them to control and exploit the states for its own benefit.

All four of the speeches that make up these debates are fairly dense and can be difficult to follow, considering that the attitude towards and management of public lands is very different in the modern day than it was almost a hundred and eighty years ago. What I want to focus on is the way that Webster – considered one of America's greatest orators and debaters – follows Haynes' organization when he constructs his own reply.

Webster:

1. The federal government is not selling land at high prices for exactly the reasons mentioned.
2. The federal government has not exploited anyone and certainly has not treated the western settlers at all like England treated Ireland.
3. If the federal government uses these lands for revenue, it will not be overstepping its constitutional bounds, and the states will benefit.
4. The responsibility of the sale of public land should remain with the federal government to encourage American expansion into the west.

This method of point-by-point refutation is easy to follow and effective. It allows you to ensure that you have answered all your opponent's arguments completely.

Taking Advantage of a Disorganized Opponent

While you will still have to make a good argument, and build your own credibility, pointing out that your opponent does not have an organized argument can be of great advantage to you.

Many people argue off the top of their head and do not take time to think about why they believe the things they are saying. Often, they will try to argue by repeating taglines they found on the Internet about their pet topics. These are by nature disorganized – since they are meant to make people who already believe the thing feel good about their beliefs, not to convince others by any kind of reasonable argument. You don't have to be confrontational to reveal the flaws and gaps in their reasoning, just ask for a logical progression in their argument.

If the information does not seem to relate to the subject at hand, ask, "What does K have to do with E?" For example: "What does oil field workers loving their families have to do with the refusal to develop clean energy?" Your opponent might have a reason for connecting the two, but chances are, they haven't thought it through.

If it seems that they made a jump in reasoning ask, "Why does A necessarily lead to F?" You can effectively pin someone in a bad argument just by asking for clarification. For example: "Why does holding a pro-life position mean that someone wants women to be slaves or dead?"

If it seems that they are contradicting themselves, point out the contradiction and ask them to explain it. "It seems to me that you cannot hold idea A and idea B at the same time. Can you explain your reasoning?" This either gives your opponent a chance to clarify a misunderstanding – which will prevent the argument from disintegrating into a purposeless conflict – or reveal their own inconsistency, which creates problems for their ability to prove their point.

Now that we have seen how to start an argument, and how to organize the body of the argument, we can move on to the most fun part: bringing it all together for a powerful conclusion.

Chapter 3: Compelling Conclusions

A good conclusion presents your argument as something proved beyond reasonable doubt. It is also the last thing you get to say in the course of the argument or the debate, so you want to leave it ringing in your listener's ears.

Basic Structure of Conclusions

A conclusion should tie up all the loose ends in your argument. As you reach the end of your argument, make sure to answer any questions you raised earlier in the argument. If you are writing a paper, look back through it and see if you promised closure of certain topics to your reader. If you raised problems, provide solutions, or compelling reasons why you cannot provide solutions. Do not introduce any new information at this point; only use whatever you brought up already.

Review the basic outline of your arguments. Remind your audience of the progression of thought so that they can clearly see why the argument you set up leads logically to this particular conclusion.

Reiterate your proof. Remember that you probably already know your conclusion since you want to argue for it. At the beginning of the argument, we stated the conclusion as a thing that still needs to be proved. Now that you spent some time proving it, you can present your conclusion as a proven fact. Be careful, especially in writing, not to plagiarize yourself by just repeating your original proof word for word.

Keep your conclusion short compared to the extent of your argument. A concise argument may only need a conclusion of two or three sentences, while the average argument and essay may need a paragraph, perhaps two, for an especially long piece.

Finishing a Progression of Thought

In the last chapter, I talked about logical progression of thought. Conclusion ends that progression. In the course of your argument, you will make many mini-conclusions as you work through each proof. Your main conclusion will come out of summary of these sets of conclusions. It can be helpful to think of this as if you are a lawyer calling for the jury to make a particular verdict.

This example comes from the famous Supreme Court case of Marbury vs. Madison, which confirmed the right of the judiciary branch to void acts of Congress if they are unconstitutional:

Because Congress is limited by the Constitution in its legislative power, and;

Because those limits would be meaningless if they cannot be enforced, and;

Because the Supreme Court is placed by law in a position to examine the constitutionality of any legislation put out by Congress.

Therefore, the Supreme Court has the legal power to declare an act of Congress unconstitutional and therefore void.

Written by Chief Justice John Marshall, this particular ruling – the conclusion of the court upon hearing a particular set of evidence and providing their analysis of it – defined the powers and influence of the Supreme Court up to the present day. Such is the power of a well-defined progression of thought.

Bringing Home the Proof

State your conclusion in the strongest terms possible. Avoid hesitant phraseology such as, "I think that…" and "It is possible to say that…" and "It is my opinion…" By this time, your argument should have taken your conclusion beyond the hemisphere of possibility and opinion and into a statement of fact. Example:

Considering the information above, it is possible – and I think reasonable – to conclude that David Hume's skepticism might go a little too far. In my opinion, he misses a connection between perception and reality that I think really exists. Our ability to function in the world means that we can probably perceive it accurately, for the most part, at least Thomas Reid seems to think so.

This conclusion might follow from the argument, but it gives us no reason to embrace it. Even if the rest of the paper or speech were well-argued, this conclusion would fall flat, like a limp handshake. The speaker does not exude any confidence in their own conclusion, and that confidence will help your audience to believe that you are indeed right.

Let's have our writer try again:

Considering the information above, we can confidently conclude that David Hume takes skepticism too far. He misses a critical connection between perception and reality that really exists and allows us to function in the world. Our ability to gather empirical data should give us confidence that we can know how the world works, not cast it into doubt.

Because we worked so hard earlier in the argument to follow a logical train of thought and not make any assumptions, we are completely justified in making strong statements at the end of the argument.

Once you have summarized your argument and presented your logical conclusion as proven, you need to conclude the conclusion. Strong conclusions finish off with calls to action, possible consequences of the conclusion, and ringing rhetorical questions. Your audience wants to know where they are now, and what they should do with all the information you just presented to them.

Historian and philosopher David Hume ended his Enquiry Concerning Human Understanding with this powerful call to action:

"If we take in our hand any volume; of divinity or school metaphysics, for instance; let us ask, *does it contain any experimental reasoning concerning quantity or number?* No. *Does it contain any experimental reasoning concerning matter of fact and existence?* No. Commit it then to the flames: For it can contain nothing but sophistry and illusion."

We can see Hume's confidence in this conclusion; not only is he right, but the things which he disproved are useful only as kindling. Where is the audience? In a place where they can judge the usefulness of different ideas. What should they do? Reject all that do not deal with math or matters of fact and existence. Karl Marx ends his Communist Manifesto with equal force:

"Let the ruling classes tremble at a Communistic revolution. The proletarians have nothing to lose but their chains. They have a world to win. WORKING MEN OF ALL COUNTRIES, UNITE!"

Where is the audience? The proletariat is on the verge of freedom and can lose nothing in their quest for it. The bourgeoisie is faced with a working class who will no longer endure their excesses. What should they do? The proletariat should unite and take their freedom, as the bourgeoisie tremble at the overwhelming power of the working man.

Whether or not you agree with Hume and Marx, we can see the strength and confidence they exude. We know especially that Marx's call to action proved successful since Communist Revolutions rocked Europe soon after he published the document in 1848. They left those who read their conclusions with no doubt as to where they stood and what they ought to do about it.

Countering Poor Conclusions

A poor conclusion provides you an excellent opportunity to deconstruct your opponent's argument. You can do this in several ways: show that their premises actually lead to your conclusion, reveal a contradiction between their premises and their conclusions, or show that their conclusion is invalid given their own argument.

A good example of the first comes from the debate between creationists and evolutionists over the interpretation of the age of rock layers. Both groups present the same information about the number of layers in a given piece of rock, their condition, location, and the kind of rock in which they were found. The creationist will use all of this information to claim that the rock is relatively young and that the layers were formed quickly, perhaps during a global flood. The evolutionist will counter that according to this information, the layers built up over long periods of time, and therefore the rock must be ancient. Each claim that his opponent's data proves his own point. If they do use exactly the same data set, the one who writes the most compelling conclusion is likely to win over the audience.

Sometimes people's conclusions completely contradict all of the information they gave during their argument. This often happens when someone is determined to come to a particular conclusion in spite of the evidence. If you see these kinds of contradictions, point them out for your own benefit.

Finally, some arguments don't prove their conclusion. This can happen when someone switches subjects mid-argument through ignorance or poor reasoning. For example:

Salmon populations in the Northwest are shrinking dangerously, despite efforts at rehabilitation of their habitats.

Conclusion: We should put limits on cod fishing, so the cod don't go extinct.

Unless the argument compared salmon and cod from the beginning, this conclusion does not follow the argument. It might be true, but we have no way of knowing if the situation of the cod is anywhere close to that of the salmon. If you pay attention to your opponent's argument all the way through, this mistake will be obvious, and you can point it out. As always, be careful to keep good track of your own thread of argument so that you do not fall into these mistakes.

Chapter 4: Watch Your Language!

Anger is never without an argument, but seldom with a good one.

-Indira Gandhi

One of the biggest barriers to winning an argument is not the strength of your ideas, but the way in which you present yourself. Many people try to win arguments by making the other person feel intimidated or guilty, but this will make your opponent angry and put them on the defensive. They may ignore many good points you make just out of spite. If you are arguing with someone for the benefit of others – like a public debate – the audience may side with your opponent because they feel he has been unfairly treated. Your attitude can make or break your success as a debater.

Earlier, we briefly touched on the kind of language you ought to use – when I talked about treating opponents with respect. You should come across as attentive, fair-minded, and rational. Treat the opposition as a person. Don't stoop to the level of a boorish opponent; you can't beat a pig in a mud-slinging contest.

The best way to look attentive is to be attentive. Don't interrupt; instead, listen to what your opponent has to say. Try to understand where they are coming from and take the time to clarify things you don't understand. Taking the time to hear them out and understand their argument will give you the best chance of countering their points effectively.

Be fair-minded. If your opponent says something right, grant them that point. If you are in a formal debate, you'll want to stick to your argument to the bitter end, even if your opponent gets some points on you. In everyday discourse, however, allow yourself to admit when you might be wrong, or when you might not have an answer for some point the other person presents. Even if you disagree with someone, not everything they say will be irrational. Acknowledge a reasonable argument when you see one.

If your opponent becomes confrontational, strive your best not to respond in kind, especially if you need to appeal to an audience. A calm person trying to have a rational discussion with a wild-eyed fanatic is a kind of argument in itself. As I'll talk about later, you can make yourself more convincing without changing a single argument by changing the way you present yourself and your argument.

Avoid threatening language. Trying to intimidate your opponent will not win you an argument because it does not make one. You want to win the argument because you are right, not because you can scare someone into pretending to agree with you.

You may see protesters shouting people down or chanting to express their opinions. While this behavior is forceful, it does not provide a single good argument. Anyone who disagrees with the protesters is only further encouraged to see them as irrational. Getting up in someone's face or demanding that they answer you immediately or mocking them or interrupting them, or answering for them before they get a chance to speak, are all examples of intimidation. None of them work in your favor. Always treat your opponent – and their ideas – with respect. Let them be the ones to embarrass themselves.

Sarcasm is fun, but it isn't an argument. Using your opponent as the butt of a joke might make you feel good, but it provides no real support for your case. Let's take this hypothetical example:

Opponent: I don't really think global warming matters.

You: Oh, you just want to watch the world burn, huh?

O: I'm just not sure—

Y: Polar bears are *dying*, you heartless jerk!

O: No, they're not!

Y: Do you live under a rock?

If this looks like bullying, it might be because it is. Rather than resorting to intimidation or cheap jokes, take a second to find out their reasoning, and attack that instead:

Opponent: I don't really think global warming matters.

You: Why not?

O: The climate changes all the time. You know, seasons and stuff.

Y: Seasonal changes aren't the same as climate change. Historically, changes in temperature have disrupted weather patterns and forced whole groups of people to move out of their homelands.

Now you are set up with a statement of fact, your opponent does not feel threatened, and you can proceed with your argument. Remember, we are using logic, and a good logical argument like the one you just learned to make can be incredibly overwhelming on its own. You do not need to posture to make it stronger.

Avoid arguments driven by emotion. Feelings, while real, do not constitute proof. Emotional arguments make people feel sad or guilty but will not necessarily convince anyone that what you are saying is true. At worst, they will make them angry or defensive, especially if you imply that they are a cruel or careless person. Your argument should not be with the person, but with their ideas. You can imply that the idea is unethical or otherwise deeply flawed without claiming that your opponent is a bad person.

One of the most common examples of emotional arguments appears in advertising. Political ads show the ugliest pictures of their opponents with frightening music playing in the background. Men's razor commercials feature beautiful women tenderly stroking the man's freshly shaved jawline. Clothing and electronics ads show people who are happy and cool using their products. All of these appeal to the emotions: fear, the desire to be attractive, or the hope that getting the right clothes will make us popular. While these feelings are powerful motivators (the people who develop these ads aren't paid well for nothing), they possess about as much substance as a stick of cotton candy: fun and attractive, but ultimately empty. You should engage with your audience's emotions, but you should find a way to do it without compromising the logical integrity of your argument.

Don't create caricatures of your opposition. A caricature exaggerates a feature to the extreme, and while many writers use it as a powerful literary device, it does not help structure a sound argument because it deals with a hypothetical extreme rather than a reality. Examples of caricature include Ebenezer Scrooge (greedy capitalist) in Charles Dickens' *A Christmas Carol* and Shylock (usurious Jew) in Shakespeare's *Measure for Measure*. Both are the work of talented writers and perform their function well, but neither one represents his group exactly. This mistake in argumentation is similar to the logical fallacies of Strawman and Hasty Generalization. If you create a caricature, you will come across as dismissive, and even ignorant. In a debate, take your opponent's ideas as they are and work to counter them in their real form.

As you can see, presentation and language play a powerful role in making a good argument. We will come back to these ideas later when we talk about logical fallacies and also go into detail about presenting yourself in person and through your writing.

Chapter 5: Mastering the Art of Analogy

Analogies compare things to explain or clarify them. Good analogies can help you deal with complex subjects and help others understand the importance of something they had not thought of before. They can even be used to prove your argument. In this chapter, we will look at how to structure analogies and how to avoid the logical fallacy of the false analogy.

An analogy is not quite the same thing as a metaphor. A metaphor describes its object using a term which is not literally applicable: i.e., "My brother is my rock." Analogy compares one thing to another for the purpose of proof or explanation. It can turn the abstract into something concrete and thus avoids demanding strenuous mental gymnastics from your audience.

The first part of making a good analogy is to know your audience. Use concrete terms and examples that they already know and understand. An analogy drawn from baking, for example, might not go over well with a group of mechanics because they would not understand it.

Next, try to match as many elements of the analogy as possible to the elements of the idea you want to explain. The more matches, the better the analogy will be. Still, strive for simplicity. A good analogy makes an idea less complex and easier to understand; be careful not to bog your audience down in trying to understand the analogy itself.

We already have some familiar analogies in our language: *like finding a needle in a haystack* and as *useful as rearranging deck chairs on the Titanic*. But what if you want to make up your own analogies?

Look for examples in real life and your own experiences that are common across many people groups. One popular analogy comes from the Biblical book of Matthew, where Jesus likens hypocrisy to a whitewashed tomb: Just like a new washed tomb *looks* nice but hides decaying bodies on its inside, a hypocrite puts on a good face but is something else entirely.

Analogies can work for you in many different ways. Use an analogy when your topic does not lend itself to easy explanation. Something highly technical or abstract often avoids the understanding of people who are not already familiar with it. Using an analogy puts the idea into terms they can understand. One popular example is the explanation of governmental systems using cows:

Feudalism: You have two cows. The lord of the manor takes some of the milk and all of the cream.

Socialism: You have two cows. The government takes one cow and gives it to your neighbor. You are both forced to join a cooperative where you have to teach your neighbor how to take care of his cow.

Dictatorship: You have two cows. The government takes both and shoots you.

This analogy, while amusing, also provides an easy way to remember the basics of governmental systems and the differences between them. It serves better for an easy-to-grasp explanation than grappling through the terminology and nuance of political theory.

Some analogies add beauty and color and a poetic element to your speaking or writing. In the essay, "Meditation in a Toolshed", C.S.

Lewis uses the analogy of looking *along* a beam of light and looking *at* a beam of light to discuss the difference between experiencing something and observing the experience of something. Not only does it give a concrete example of the abstract concept, but it adds an element of grace to the writing that would not otherwise exist and increases the reader's enjoyment.

Other analogies make powerful arguments of themselves if they can effectively liken a simple or well-known situation to a more convoluted one. These can turn into extended stories. One of the oldest is Aesop's fable, "The Boy Who Cried Wolf":

"A bored Boy tending Sheep cried "Wolf!" to get attention. He did it again, and people came. A third time and the Boy was ignored. Goodbye, flock.

A liar will not be believed, even when telling the truth."

In this story, we see the analogy working as a proof. It follows a logical line of thought: Lie to people, they stop believing you. When they stop believing you, it no longer matters if you are telling the truth; they will not believe you. Analogies like this present material in a simple and profound form, making it near impossible not to grasp. If you can use common experience to tell a simple story that reflects the idea you want to argue for, you will be using one of the hardest hitting proofs in rhetoric.

A good analogy, once made, does its work extremely well. As you enjoy making your analogies, however, beware the specter of the false analogy. Unlike a bad analogy, which simply falls short of its purpose or fails to resonate with its audience, a false analogy assumes that because two things are similar in one way, they must also be similar in another way. For example:

People who cannot go without their morning coffee are no different than alcoholics.

While there appears to be a similarity – people seeking a particular drink every day and both coffee and alcohol being addictive – there are significant enough differences between coffee addiction and alcoholism that this analogy does not hold up as an effective argument.

Another example of false analogy takes the structure: A is like B. Because some Bs are C, then A has to be C. Example:

That man is wearing a balaclava. Bank robbers wear balaclavas; therefore, that man must be a bank robber.

This false analogy ignores the fact that, although some bank robbers wear balaclavas, the head cloth is also a common part of cold-weather gear meant to protect the face from the wind and snow. The man could be a robber, or he could be an outdoorsman who doesn't want a frostbitten nose. The balaclava is not sufficient for us to tell the difference.

Here is a common false analogy in this form:

Being punched is painful. Having someone disagree with you is painful. Therefore, if someone disagrees with you, it's just like they punched you in the face.

Just one similarity – pain in this case – is insufficient to make an analogy. You need several, all of which are easily obvious and assist in making an explanation. If you need the analogy to make an argument, check it against the rules for a logical progression of thought that we already learned, and make sure you don't make any leaps in reasoning.

Analogies are powerful tools for explaining difficult concepts, adding vividness to your language and even making proofs. When making analogies, be sure you use examples that your audience understands. Look for similarities between the concept and the analogy and try to create an analogy that reflects the concept as strongly as possible.

Finally, don't be afraid to use an analogy as a proof – just construct it soundly and watch it do the heavy lifting.

Chapter 6: Burden of Proof – Convince Them You're Right

A well-structured argument is critical to winning any kind of debate, but, as we have seen so far, it only covers the very basics of making an argument logical and consistent. A lot goes into convincing someone that you are right. In this chapter, we will look at different ways to provide support for a logical progression of thought.

Isn't Logic Enough?

People do not just believe an idea because they found it to be logical; they believe in the idea because they like it. Blaise Pascal said that there are two ways by which we accept opinions: the understanding (we realized that they are true) and the will (we want them to be true). The most common, he said, was that of the will – "For all men are almost led to believe not of proof, but by attraction." As a scientist, this troubled Pascal; the ways of getting a person to like a thing were as many and varied as people themselves and had nothing to do with whether a proposition was true. The best advice he could give was to know your audience – what he or she likes, and what he or she thinks is true, and then demonstrate that your idea is by these.

Like Pascal, I know of no hard and fast rules to make your argument winsome to everyone. Thankfully for us, people are reasonable as well as emotional. If you civilly present yourself and refrain from purposefully insulting either your opponent or your audience, you are well on your way to convincing them that you are right.

Convincing Structure

While we will go over this in more detail when we talk specifically about oral and written arguments, we do need a little bit more on the structure to continue.

Open with a thesis: that which you want to prove. Next, provide relevant statements of fact and definitions. If you are walking through an extended proof, put the steps in their proper chronological order. This looks like, *Because A, therefore B. Because B, therefore C. Because C, therefore D.*

The other way to support your thesis is to provide many reasons why it is true. This looks like, *Because A, therefore D. Because B, therefore D. Because C, therefore D.*

Both these structures are effective and will present your argument coherently and convincingly. We will talk more about choosing between them when we discuss deductive and inductive reasoning.

Inviting Agreement

You can invite agreement just by your attitude, which shows whether you are speaking directly to your audience or writing to them. Avoid mocking your opponent or using them as the butt of jokes. Sarcasm and satire are powerful tools, but they are tools of criticism through hyperbole. They can reveal problems and speak to universal truths, but they do not make for strong arguments because they tend to be negative in nature. An important element of argumentation is to be positive: not in an optimistic sense, but in that you are arguing *for* something, not just pointing out flaws.

If your opponent begins to bully you, or if you are responding in writing to a personal attack, refrain from making personal attacks in return. Point out your opponent's rudeness and show that their attack adds nothing to the discussion but remain composed. Be confident in who you are and be confident in the strength of your argument. Personal attacks and petty insults are the domain of uncertain and frightened people. If they have to go after you, they have already lost the debate.

Even if your opponent has better points than you, if they present them while screaming and stomping their feet, you can come out on top by staying sane. As a debater, you ought not to make the argument that if someone is rude, their ideas are bad, but your audience is likely to make that argument for you. "How could that person be right?" they will ask themselves. "They're practically foaming at the mouth, and almost all they can do is scream insults, while this person over here is actually trying to make a rational argument."

Causative Arguments

A causative argument claims that one thing caused another. There are two ways to use informal causative reasoning: relevant difference and common thread.

A relevant difference requires at least two circumstances to argue it. You have probably already used this during troubleshooting. If you aren't getting a result that you want, you change your process one thing at a time until you find the thing that makes the difference and causes the result that you want. This is the relevant difference. For example:

I made my coffee today just the same as every other day, except I used a different coffee brand. Usually, my coffee tastes good, but today it was terrible! That brand of coffee must not be any good.

The change in coffee brands is the relevant difference because it is the only thing that changed, so it is logical to assume it had a direct effect on the flavor of the coffee.

A difference is only relevant when it is directly tied to the process of cause and effect under examination. Examine the difference to see if it can possibly have any kind of real effect on the process. There may be other differences, but they may not be relevant.

Superstition is an excellent example of a faulty causative argument. Ancient peoples without any knowledge of the real causes of seasons and weather patterns performed complex rituals to bring about ideal conditions because they believed that their ritual was the relevant difference:

Every year we perform our ritual dance and sacrifice a goat to bring the summer rain for our crops. This year we performed our ritual dance, but we did not sacrifice a goat. The rain did not come. The reason the rain did not come was that we did not sacrifice a goat.

While we might know more about the scientific causes of droughts as moderns, we still sometimes use this same flawed reasoning:

My favorite team won five games in a row, and I wore my #18 jersey every time. However, last week, I wore a regular shirt, and they lost. I must wear my #18 jersey so that they will win.

No matter how much we know that wearing a different shirt doesn't really change the outcome, we will probably wear the jersey just for good luck. When constructing a tight argument, though, do your research. Examine the common elements between different events thoroughly before claiming a relevant difference.

The other kind of causative reasoning is common thread reasoning. This is when a feature appears over several cases, and a certain event or element is present every time. Once again, you've probably used this in troubleshooting. Example:

No matter whom we elect to the City Council, the city always has the same problems of inefficiency and poor infrastructure. But even though we elect new people to the City Council, the policy hasn't ever changed. Therefore, the problem is with the policies, not the council members.

Take care when using this argument to make sure that you identified the relevant common thread. For example:

Every time I go to work somewhere, I get laid off within a few months. I've driven the same car to work every time. I must be getting laid off because of my car.

Although the car is a commonality between all the situations, it probably is not directly connected to getting laid off, any more than the commonality of tying your shoes each morning. Make sure that the difference you identify is connected as a potential cause of the effect.

How to Make the Data Work for You

Let's talk about data. Many people see a presentation of data as an end-all argument just by itself. However, data is complicated and by nature subject to all kinds of interpretations. Different people can put a different spin on an identical statistic.

Data comes from an analysis of a particular population. You need to know who gathered that data, how, and what population it came from. For instance, if I did a study of white-on-black racism in the United States and pulled my entire population of people interviewed from KKK and Neo-Nazi rallies, my data, while entirely accurate, would not offer a good cross-section of the US population. If I chose 100,000 people randomly from all different places in the US, I might get a good cross-section, but if I asked poor questions like, "Have you ever disliked any person of color?" then I would not provide accurate data at all, because a person may dislike another person for reasons which are not racial.

If your opponent's argument draws from a poorly conducted study – poor population sample and flawed methods – you can use that to discredit them. But what if their data comes from a good study?

See if they applied it correctly. In the above example, the data I pulled together on racism by interviewing people at KKK and Neo-Nazi rallies applies to the attitudes of avowed white-supremacist groups. I would be wrong to apply it to the entire population of the United States because the sample did not represent the country well.

Challenge their cause and effect. People usually use data and statistics to argue cause and effect. As we learned in the last chapter, however, many different causes can be applied to one effect. One particularly hot topic at the moment is global warming. While the data clearly shows a warming trend, estimates as to the extent to which humans contribute to global warming range from 0-100%, with no clear consensus among scientists. In their debates, these scientists don't argue whether global warming exists but rather what its causes are.

Give the data a different spin. Raw data requires context to understand it, and you can manipulate the message the data send to your audience by changing its context. For example:

According to the FBI, the rate of violent crime is up 4% from last year to this year; crime must be getting worse, right? However, violent crime has actually fallen by 12% in the last nine years, and rates of burglary are down by almost 30%.

Presenting Examples

Examples take your ideas out of the abstract into something concrete that people can see or experience directly. When you demonstrate using real-world examples, your audience sees that your ideas are not only theoretical but are drawn from events and experiences. Like analogies, you should use examples when talking about difficult concepts. If you can find a real-live example of your theory in action, then present it. Examples provide weight and help to demonstrate concepts that would otherwise be up for debate. Personal stories, statistics, historical events, and results from experiments all provide plenty of fodder for building examples.

Use personal stories to relate to your audience. These can be profound or funny and give your audience the feeling of knowing you as a person, which can make them interested in listening to what you want to say:

"When my daughter chose to dust off the little girl who had pulled her hair a few minutes before, a realized that a six-year-old child knew more about the power of forgiveness than I did."

Historical events provide examples for looking at the consequences of long-term governmental, social, and economic policy. It can also provide insight into environmental impact and agriculture:

Attempting to get revenge on a country after defeating it in a war has terrible consequences for both sides. When the Allies defeated Germany in World War I, they demanded inordinate reparations, then hamstrung the German economy's ability to raise the capital to pay those reparations. The suffering and resentment caused by this mistake led directly to World War II.

An example from history is especially compelling because the event really happened. Like analogies, however, you should be careful to make sure that your example matches the process of whatever theory you want to describe. Each component should be in direct relation to a historical component. Look carefully for extra components that could render the example irrelevant to your argument.

Despite how data can be manipulated, it still makes for excellent support for your argument. Citing data and statistics from studies relevant to your topic provides the extra force of experiment. It is one thing if all of these are your own inventions; it's another if a great many studies done by a diverse group of people either come to your same conclusion or provide evidence that your conclusion is sound.

Use studies conducted by reputable sources that people trust. Don't use your own data unless you are an expert in your field and can speak with command on the topic.

Authorities and Experts

The use of examples takes us to the consultation of authorities and experts. Chances are, you do not have many years of experience and a degree in the topic of your argument, but the Internet gives us access to millions of people who do. Take advantage of it. It is one thing for you to say that college is overpriced for what it offers in terms of opportunity, but if you can find a former head of the Department of Education who agrees with you, your argument packs a stronger punch.

When choosing your authorities, look for well-known names in the topic. Quoting Albert Einstein, for instance, would bring weight to an argument on quantum mechanics. Other weighty names include Bertrand Russel, Alexis de Tocqueville, and Stephen Hawking. All these people bring their reputation with them, and their support for your argument – or against the argument of your opponent – will help convince your audience that you ought to be believed.

Another sign of expertise comes from the reputation of a particular position: Dean of Harvard Law School, Nobel Prize Winner, and Chief Justice of the Supreme Court. All these positions are known to be held by highly qualified people and can give them significance in the minds of your audience even if they do not recognize the person's name.

Avoid pulling experts from outside the topic. Just because someone is a well-known scientist does not mean that they are an expert in history. Make sure their reputation applies directly to the argument you want to make.

Another place to find experts is from reputable publishers: Oxford University Press, Pew Research, The Stanford Encyclopedia of Philosophy, or the Federal Bureau of Investigation. These organizations and others are known and respected for their high-quality material and their rigorous standards. Peer-reviewed journals and studies will also provide you with excellent content for your research as well as support.

Why You Should Counter Your Own Argument

Rather than waiting for your opponent to counter you, bring up the dissenting opinion yourself. This can be the scariest part of an argument because it requires you to understand and honestly present the other side. What if your audience thinks that the other side is better, or more reasonable? While it is tempting to avoid bringing up the opposition yourself, it makes your argument stronger because you not only bring up counter-points but also address them.

There are a couple of ways of doing this. The first is to anticipate your audience's questions. What might someone who disagreed with you say? What kind of doubts would someone have that need to be addressed before they can embrace your argument as true? For example:

Recent events have made it clear that filibustering does more harm than good. But isn't filibustering important? Doesn't it provide a tool for a minority group in the Senate or House to hold off a decision until public outcry can turn the tide of the majority?

It certainly used to. However, more and more, filibustering no longer serves its intended purpose. It wastes important time and holds laws hostage by the people's elected representatives.

To make such an argument, I would want to bring in some reputable sources and significant recent examples. But by introducing the opposition myself, I inform my audience that I am aware of their possible doubts and am willing to address them, which increases their trust in me and what I have to say.

The second way of bringing up the opposition is to comment on arguments you discovered in the course of your research on your topic. Experts do not often agree, and the deeper you go into your topic, the more debate you will find. Present the opposing view and then show how you and your supporting experts refute that view:

Sigmund Freud's breakthrough research at the turn of the 20th Century revolutionized psychology and created psychoanalysis. His research focused on the progression of human sexuality and the problems caused by the inability to reconcile the stages of sexual phases. Modern research, however, has shown that many psychological problems that Freud blamed on failure to reconcile sexual stages are really caused by other factors – or even that they are not problems at all.

Always present the opposition in the fairest way possible. If you are responding directly to an opponent, take the time to make sure you have understood their argument. When you build up the opposition well, it makes you all the more believable when you tear down their argument.

Chapter 7: The Art of Deduction (and Induction)

We usually use two types of arguments: deductive and inductive. Both form the foundation for excellent arguments and offer compelling proof. While you can use either one to great effect, they are more powerful in particular niches. You might also be especially good at one or the other.

Deductive Reasoning

In its simplest form, deductive reasoning begins with cause and proceeds to explain the effects. It moves from generalities into specifics, with the specifics being a necessary conclusion from the general truths. We use deductive reasoning frequently in mathematics. For example:

Using the truth that things which are equal to the same thing are equal to each other, then if A=B and B=C, then A=C.

All cats are felines. Fluffy is a cat. Therefore, Fluffy is a feline.

The weakness of deductive reasoning is the same as its strength: it depends on the truth of its premises because the conclusion is already on the premises.

If all ships float, and the Mary Beth is a ship, then the conclusion that the Mary Beth floats is already in the premises, it just hasn't been independently stated yet.

Your premises restrict you in a couple of ways when making deductive arguments. They have to contain your conclusion already, and they have to be indisputable. If I can demonstrate that all ships do not float, then the conclusion that the Mary Beth floats must be called into question.

Be careful of invalid deductions. An invalid deduction assumes that the specific thing lands in a closed category when that category might apply to several different things:

All owls have talons.

Wheeler has talons.

Therefore, Wheeler is an owl.

None of the premises, in this case, are untrue, but they have been misapplied to the conclusion because the conclusion is not a logical necessity. Other animals besides owls have talons, so 'has talons' does not tell us whether or not a specific creature is an owl.

Everyone living in Chicago lives in Ohio.

Kate lives in Ohio.

Therefore, Kate lives in Chicago.

Once again, while none of the premises are untrue, the conclusion I drew was not a logical necessity, because other conclusions could be drawn. Kate could live in Columbus, and the premises would still be true.

Use deductive arguments when you need to build proofs on top of one another to reach your conclusion. Use the methods we have learned in the previous chapters to support your premises, and you can build a conclusion which is not only reasonable but an absolute logical necessity.

Inductive Reasoning

Inductive reasoning induces causes from an examination of the effects by moving from specific cases to general ideas. Think of a scientist drawing conclusions after doing many experiments. We use induction to notice patterns in results or behaviors. This kind of reasoning works well when you want to argue a general principle from a set of events or conclusions.

A teacher notices that his students engage eagerly during a discussion-heavy class. The next week, he tries incorporating discussion again, although the topic is different. The students engage eagerly once again. The teacher concludes that his class engages with a subject when they have an opportunity for discussion.

You may notice some similarities between this and the idea of a common thread that we looked at with causative reasoning. That is because we use inductive reasoning to find a common thread. Use inductive reasoning when you present a series of proofs for one conclusion:

When I eat cookies, I feel sick. When I eat sandwiches, I feel sick. When I eat pizza, I feel sick. When I eat cake, I feel sick. The common ingredient between all of these is flour; I must be gluten intolerant.

The weakness in inductive reasoning is that it relies on empirical information and is therefore subject to limitations. For example:

Every cat I have ever seen is either black or white.

Therefore, all cats are black or white.

While all the information you have points to cats only being black or white, someone who has more information could quickly disprove you by bringing in their pet tabby. When you use an inductive argument, draw from a broad selection of proofs. Use information from other people, and don't depend on your own experience.

The famous scientist Sir Isaac Newton used an inductive argument to prove the existence of gravity. For thousands of years, people thought that items fell to Earth because it was in their nature to fall to the surface of the Earth. They thought that planets went around the Earth and later the Sun because they were in concentric rotating spheres, or because they floated on an invisible sea of ether.

Newton noticed that the centrifugal force exercised on a rotating sling was the same as the force with which the moons of Jupiter were kept in rotation around their planet. Then he noticed that the math showed that the force with which all the planets were kept in rotation around the sun was the same. Finally, the ratios of this force were not just equal between planets and their moons, but between planets, moons, and objects dropped on the surface of the Earth. From these observations, he concluded that one force must act on all these bodies. While our view of gravity has changed in the following centuries, scientists still believe that whatever keeps the planets in motion is the same force that controls the tides and makes coffee mugs fall when we drop them.

Newton and many other scientists after him used inductive reasoning to find the common thread between seemingly unrelated events, and many of their conclusions still stand. They were careful when gathering their data, and worked hard to ensure that they chose common threads that made sense and could explain everything as simply as possible.

Because scientists tend to prefer to use inductive reasoning, inductive reasoning is popularly considered to be inherently scientific and therefore well accepted as a good standard for proving an argument. It can be more appealing than deductive reasoning since modern society tends to be skeptical of axioms.

Chapter 8: Sophistry! Identifying Logical Fallacies

Logical fallacies can sound nice, but they do not support an argument. While pointing out a logical fallacy is not an argument in and of itself, pointing out that your opponent used a logical fallacy can weaken their propositions and set the stage for you to counter them with your own proofs.

Slippery Slope

If A happens, then Z will happen. A slippery slope argument jumps to conclusions with nothing to support the connection. Example:

If the city bans the sale of 24 oz. sodas, eventually they will ban the sale of any soda at all. We should not let them ban the sale of 24 oz sodas.

If I fail this class, I won't ever be able to make it up, I won't graduate college, and I'll die homeless in a gutter somewhere because I did not get a job.

Watch for this fallacy when taking an idea to its natural conclusion. Remember to use a step-by-step progression. If your opponent uses a slippery slope fallacy, use the opportunity to demonstrate that their conclusion is invalid. You might note that the city is not preventing people from buying soda, just a certain size container; everyone can still buy and drink their soda as they please. Failing one class does not destroy a person's opportunities of ever acquiring a job.

Hasty Generalization

Hasty generalization occurs when someone moves too quickly through an inductive argument. For example:

The first two stores I went to did not have eggs. Therefore, no store in this entire town has eggs.

My boyfriend cheated on me and lied about it. All men are cheats and liars.

I do not like the smell of a Sharpie. My brother does not like the smell of a Sharpie. A random woman I talked to in the airport does not like the smell of a Sharpie. No one likes the smell of a Sharpie.

When using inductive arguments, be sure to draw your conclusion from many sources or observations and avoid making sweeping claims until you have the evidence to back them up.

Post hoc ergo propter hoc

Meaning 'after this, therefore because of this,' the post hoc fallacy assumes that something is the cause of something else because it occurred before it. Just because two events happen in sequence does not mean that they are linked to one another in any way:

I washed the car, and then it rained. It rained because I washed the car.

In this case, the sequence of events – car washing and rain – have no connection to one another. Sometimes the events appear to be linked together, however:

Yesterday, I used my truck to help my friends move. Today, I have a flat tire. I must have gotten a flat tire because we loaded the truck bed so heavily.

While there could be a link here, it is uncertain. The truck could have hit a curb and damaged a tire valve or run over a nail during an unrelated trip to the grocery store.

When countering this fallacy, suggest alternative conclusions, or show that the events are not connected.

Genetic Fallacy

Genetic fallacy analyzes the truth of a claim by the origins of the premises:

This man is a Christian. Any defense he makes of Christianity is inherently biased and therefore wrong because he wants Christianity to be true.

Another example of this in the present day is the misidentification of entire news outlets as 'fake news', rather than realizing that individual stories are fake news when they lie about or exaggerate situations into falsehood:

CNN presented this news story. Last week, CNN presented a story which was proven to be badly researched and incorrect. Therefore, this story must also be badly researched and incorrect.

The source of a premise does not necessarily make it true or false. A person with a long habit of truth can lie, and vice verse. Examine the claim itself, independent of the source. If you are having trouble because of a personal bias, ask yourself if you would feel better about the claim if it came from a source you trust or like. If you would, chances are you have fallen into a genetic fallacy.

If someone uses a genetic fallacy while arguing with you, direct the conversation away from the source of the premise and ask them to address the premise itself, regardless of where it came from.

Begging the Claim

Also known as begging the question, this argument is an example of poorly executed deductive reasoning:

Smoking cigarettes is deadly because smoking cigarettes can kill you.

The evidence provided for the claim assumes the claim is already true, thus begging the question: "Wait, why is that actually the case?" This is the perfect question to ask if your opponent uses this fallacy.

Argument from Incredulity

This argument assumes that because you cannot believe something, it must not be true. Example:

I can't believe that someone landed on the Moon. Therefore the Moon landing must have been faked.

There is a significant difference between your personal incredulity or ignorance, and an actual proof that something is right or wrong. Mere skepticism is not an argument unless it has support.

Either/Or

Also known as the all-or-nothing fallacy, either/or presents two opposing positions as if they are the only possible options. Example:

You don't support marriage equality. You must want to kill gay people!

If the governor doesn't take an active stance against government corruption, he must be corrupt himself.

Avoid this fallacy by paying attention to your options. Allow other people to be complex and their ideas nuanced. Just because a person does not fall into one camp does not necessarily mean that they ascribe to the other extreme.

When faced with refuting an either/or fallacy, propose a third option; don't let your opponent put you into a box.

Ad hominem

This is perhaps one of the easiest arguments to make when you are frustrated. Ad hominem attempts to attack a person's argument by attacking the person themselves:

You can't comment on policy that impacts low-income families because you have never been poor.

The only reason why you think we should keep our nuclear weapons is because you are a warmonger who can't wait for an opportunity to use them.

You only want to work on conservation in this national park because you are a tree-hugging hippie.

People of bad character, people you don't like, and people who lack experience in a topic of discussion can still say true things and make good arguments. If someone attacks you personally during an argument, don't respond in kind. Show them and your audience that you are not basing your argument on your character or knowledge but on the research you have done and the arguments you constructed.

Ad populem

The ad populem fallacy argues that because many people believe a thing, it must be true. Example:

Billions of people are religious. Being religious must be right.

This argument ignores the reality that the consensus of the majority can be wrong. Scientists, theologians, and the common people all agreed that the Earth was the center of the universe for centuries, and yet now we know it is not.

Not every consensus argument falls into the ad populem fallacy. We appeal to the majority decision of a group in law and science because the fact that a large and varied group of educated people all came to a certain conclusion is compelling. But the majority does not always land on the truth. If your opponent makes an ad populem argument, take a moment to see if anything at all can be granted from the fact that many people have this belief. Then remind your audience that the majority can be wrong and refute your opponent's argument with your own facts.

Red Herring

A red herring does not try to win an argument through fallacious reasoning; it attempts to distract you from it altogether:

"I think we should look at the benefits of raising the minimum wage."

"Raising the minimum wage? People in Africa make a lot less than you do, so why are you concerned about it?"

Suddenly, the argument goes from a discussion of the minimum wage in your country to what people in Africa are paid for their work on average.

"Why don't you support this anti-abortion legislation? We need to protect the sanctity of life in our culture."

"Why don't you support this legislation against the death penalty, then?"

Once again, this throws another, unrelated question back instead of addressing the argument. Stay on topic, and make your opponent stay on topic as best you can. If they present you with a red herring, don't let yourself become distracted. Stay with your subject and call for them to stay with the subject as well. If you're interested in the red herring, research it later.

Straw Man

The straw man fallacy distorts the opponent's argument. While this distorted argument may be easier to defeat, anyone paying attention will notice that the real argument hasn't been addressed, and they will not be convinced.

To avoid straw-manning, take the time to listen to your opponent so you can be fair to their view and represent it accurately. It might be difficult but working against their real argument will make your success all the clearer when you show that they were wrong. If someone uses straw man against you, remind them and your audience of what you really said, and proceed. Don't feel obligated to answer claims about a belief that you don't really hold.

Moral Equivalence

The fallacy of moral equivalence compares minor crimes or misdeeds with greater ones and suggests that they are equally depraved. George Orwell said that these arguments reduced to "saying that half a loaf is the same as no bread." For example:

Disagreeing with someone is basically the same thing as physically assaulting them.

The way that Israel has responded towards the Palestinians is no different than the Holocaust.

Sometimes there is a moral equivalence between things. However, they are usually the same kind of atrocity. There would be a moral equivalence between the Armenian and Rwandan Genocides for instance.

You don't have to suggest a moral equivalence to show that something is bad. The immorality of those actions or decisions can be clearly shown to anyone with an active conscience. If someone attempts to use a moral equivalence, point out the differences between the two situations. If both are examples of a crime, you don't have to defend the morality of the lesser crime to show that it is on a different plane than the greater one.

Argument by Gibberish

Argument by gibberish attempts to confuse your audience or opponent by using complex and often meaningless technical language:

According to the committee, post hoc the azimuth of the triumvir is directly cognizant of the coagment of the requirement nature and function of the slope, and if they weren't then the conclusion would be otherwise, but as it is then, we are going to go with the latter explanation.

That sentence means nothing. Don't hide an argument inside of technical language or attempt to dodge questions using fake explanations. If your opponent tries to pull something like this on you, ask for definitions and don't let them sidestep the need to really answer a question.

Argument of the Beard

The argument of the beard comes from the question of trying to figure out when the precise moment when a man goes from clean-shaven to having a beard. Also called the continuum fallacy, it assumes that because there is not a clear point where two extremes meet, there must be no difference between the two. Example:

Why can't I get my license the day before my 16th birthday? It's not as if a single day makes that much of a difference. Moreover, if a single day doesn't make that much of a difference, then a whole bunch of single days shouldn't make that much of a difference either, and I should be able to get my license when I'm fifteen.

Just because there is not a clear point of definition does not mean that two things are the same. While it might not be clear when someone goes from being clean-shaven to having a beard, any man can tell you that there is a distinct difference between the two.

Many more argumentation fallacies are out there, but these are some of the most common – with a couple of fun ones thrown in at the end. Hopefully, this list can help you avoid them yourself and know when someone tries to use them against you.

Chapter 9: Oral Arguments

Under its precise definition, an oral argument is an argument presented before a court of law. More generally, it can be used to refer to any argument conducted face-to-face.

The Art of Physical Presentation

If you know that you must present an argument ahead of time, you can prepare your appearance. For debates, business, and court wear business clothing. Even if your clothes are not particularly nice, you can still make sure that they are clean (and that you are clean). Do not dress too flamboyantly, or in clothes unfit for the situation – an evening gown at a board meeting for example. Dress your hair so people can see your face.

Because we spend so much time hunched over phones and computers, many people no longer know how to stand up straight. Standing straight will make you feel and look more confident. It will also give you more breathing room so that you don't get out of breath while talking.

To stand straight, set your feet shoulder-width apart. Don't lock your knees. Distribute your weight evenly between heels and toes. Rather than wrenching your shoulders back and sticking your chest out, lift from your ribcage and then from your collarbone. Let your shoulder blades fall down your back like a cape. Lift your chin so that the earlobe and collarbone are aligned.

Allow your hands to fall at your sides, clasp them in front of you, or let them rest on your podium – if you have one. Do not stick your hands in your pockets while making a serious argument; it will make you look sloppy. Avoid crossing your arms or planting your arms on a desk or chair. Both are closed-off stances and communicate an attempt to dominate, rather than to reason. It is acceptable to lean towards your audience while making a point.

If you are sitting down, don't splay out your knees, especially if you are wearing a skirt or a kilt. Keep your feet together, cross your ankles, or cross your legs. Sit up straight in the chair and lean forward a little if you want to communicate interest or eagerness. Don't slouch or slump down. Continue to lift from your ribcage and collarbone. Let your hands fall in your lap or rest on the arms of the chair.

Good posture radiates confidence and ease, no matter who you are or how you are dressed.

Speak clearly and distinctly. No good argument was ever communicated by mumbling. Make eye contact with people in the group as you speak and relax your arms so that you can gesture. If you do not feel comfortable making eye contact with people, find a point level with your audience's faces so that they can see your eyes.

If you have a microphone that is not attached to your head keep it at a consistent distance from your mouth. It can be intimidating to hear your voice over a set of speakers but don't yank the mic away from your face. Instead, continue to speak and allow the audio technician to adjust the volume for the audience.

Whether using a mic or not, modulate your voice to keep the pitch from going too high or low with your excitement and enthusiasm. On the flip side of this, avoid the monotone. Inflect important words and vary pitch and tone with statements and questions. If you need to read or recite a quote, gain familiarity with it and treat it as if it were spoken. Pause at commons, colons, and semicolons. Let your pitch drop at the end of statements and rise at the end of questions. Many people make the mistake of running on when reading, ignoring the punctuation and not inflecting important words. If you feel uncertain, slow down, take a breath, and try to read everything as if it were Dr. Seuss.

Interacting with Audience and Opponent

When arguing face-to-face, be ready to change tack based on the reaction of your audience. Some audiences are just stone-faced and impossible to interact with, but if you look them in the eye and speak *to* them rather than *at* them, you are on your way to engaging them in your argument. Practice in front of a mirror, or in front of other people, so you know how you look an act ahead of time.

While in a direct argument with your opponent, don't allow yourself to be intimidated. Stick to your best arguments and call out fallacies when you see them. If your opponent out-argues you on a particular point, concede. It can be painful, but showing that you are a reasonable, dynamic thinker will endear you to your audience and lend that reputation to your later arguments.

Oral Arguments in the Courtroom

If you end up in court and want to defend yourself or present a case before the judge, the argument styles you have already learned will serve you well. In court, however, you will have a limited amount of time to make your impression, so preparation is key to your success.

Write a brief for the case. A brief is a quick outline of the parties in the case and the problem to be addressed. While the final document should be about a page long, the amount of research you will need to do to create it will familiarize you with the case.

Know your court's jurisdiction. If a court does not believe they have jurisdiction in your case, they will dismiss it. Make sure you know for certain why this court has the power to make a ruling for you.

Know the relevant case law. Courts don't just use legislated law when making their rulings since legislated law cannot deal with every single situation. Issues not emphatically addressed by a particular law are subject to case law and judicial precedent. Take a look at recent cases similar to yours and see how they were ruled. Once courts begin to rule in a particular way, they tend to maintain consistency, and you can use that to your own advantage.

Don't stand up to make your argument with your hands full of papers. This goes for any argument made directly to a physical audience. By the time you argue your case before a crowd or a judge, you should know it well enough not to need notes or cue cards. You can script and memorize critical parts of your argument, such as the opening sentences and your conclusion. Memorizing an opening can keep you from stammering from nerves and give you a moment to loosen up and realize that the podium is not going to eat you alive. Speaking without papers keeps you from talking to your script and allows you to address and adapt to the current situation and audience reactions.

If you are reading this book, you clearly care about arguing well. Stand confidently on the knowledge that you have done your research and know what and how to argue to prove your case. Call your audience to listen and reason with you and watch them be convinced of your argument.

Chapter 10: Writing an Argumentative Essay

The argumentative essay is a staple of blog posts, debates, and the classroom. Knowing how to write an effective essay can boost not only the weight of your opinion but your test scores and your confidence.

Prewriting

When you sit down to write an essay, and your ideas tend to be fairly nebulous, then write down the basic idea you want to argue about and your first thoughts and reactions to it. This can be in a notebook or Word document. Get an idea of what you already know, what you need to research, and where you might stand on the topic.

My first reactions to argumentation topics tend to be visceral, so I will sometimes write a draft of my essay full of emotional reasoning, sarcasm, satire, and all kinds of other fallacies. This gets that first reaction out of my system, and I often find the seeds of arguments in the midst of my ranting. If I write something such as, 'that is just stupid,' I will go back later and ask myself why. If I can back it up, I will convert the 'that is stupid' to a more rational argument such as, 'that is contradictory because A does not equal B.'

Discover Your Thesis

Your thesis will be the thing that you argue for. It should address a topic by the length of your paper. A thesis which claims that the entirety of human knowledge is based on empirical experience will not fit in a four-page paper. Your thesis should be a single, narrow topic that fits in a sentence or two.

Bad thesis: Utilitarianism is wrong.

Good thesis: Utilitarianism depends on people learning to work towards the greatest possible good for humanity. However, social engineering cannot get people to work consistently towards the greater good. This creates a significant problem with the implementation of Utilitarianism.

Write an Outline

Your essay should be laid out on a structure similar to this:

Paragraph 1: Introduction and Thesis

Paragraph 2: Statement of Fact and Definitions

Paragraph 3: Proof 1

Paragraph 4: Proof 2

Paragraph 5: Proof 3

Paragraph 6: Counterpoints

Paragraph 7: Refutation

Paragraph 8: Conclusion

Your essay will vary with the precise structure of your argument. You may want to combine the counterpoints and refutations with their respective proofs. Some people prefer the five-paragraph essay structure:

Paragraph 1: Introduction

Paragraph 2-4: Points, counterpoints, and refutations

Paragraph 5: Conclusion

I used the five-paragraph essay all through high school to great effect and only changed methods after I got to college and needed to write much larger papers. Remember that you can always change the outline as you start to write, so don't stress over it too much, especially if you are not an outline writer.

Do Your Research

Your prewriting and your outline should give you a good idea of what you need to research. Start with keyword searches on Google or in local library databases. As you go through the relevant books and websites, record all of the information you will need for including the proper citations. Most argumentative papers require extensive citations to back them up, and you don't want to have to track down this information twice.

Your number of sources should be proportional to the size of your essay. Most argumentative essays average from four-ten pages and will not require more than three or four sources. If a teacher assigned the essay, or if the organization you write for has particular standards, check with them to find out if they have requirements for the number of sources.

Hook Your Reader

Your first sentence or two should engage the reader and make them want to see what your essay is about. A teacher once advised me to title and begin my essay as if it were the last paper he was grading at 4 a.m. My opening should be engaging enough to capture the imagination of my teacher at his most exhausted and sleep deprived.

Once you have grabbed your reader's attention, proceed with your thesis and start your transition into the main body of the essay. Don't try to make arguments in your opening paragraph. There will be plenty of time for that later.

Provide Context

Set your reader up with any information they need to know. This should take less than a page, preferably half a page. While writing this part, consider who will be reading the essay, and what information they may or may not already know. This is your statement of fact and the point where you are most likely to lose a reader. Keep it as short as possible and as interesting as possible.

Argue Your Point

Now you are down and dirty in the main body of your essay. In the thick of your argument remember to back up every claim with proof, whether directly from sources or reasoning. The methods you learned in the preceding chapters all apply here. Stay in a line of thought, and make sure that you avoid getting distracted by interesting bits of research or other 'rabbit trails'. If your essay insists upon going a particular direction, you may need to alter your thesis to match it.

Use quotes from the writers you consulted. When you use a quote, introduce the writer or speaker to your readers, and only provide the part of the quote which is most relevant to your argument. Remember, you are doing the arguing, and most of your essay should be made up of your words, not quotes for your sources.

Conclude

Wrap up all the loose ends of your argument and restate your thesis. Just as you hooked your reader at the beginning of the essay, leave them with something to think about at the end, whether a question or a call to action.

Check back through your work and make sure that you addressed any questions or problems that you raised. If you said or implied that you would deal with something, deal with it or remove it from the essay.

Edit, Edit, Edit

Congratulations, you just finished your first draft. Now go back and kick it into shape. Check for bad grammar and refine your punctuation. Cut out any hesitant language, like, "I think" or "It might".

Kill the passive voice wherever possible. One easy way to identify passive voice is to see if you can add 'by zombies' to the sentence. i.e., "It was argued… by zombies." Passive voice might not kill your argument outright but check for cases of it to see if you can change it to active voice. Chances are the change will make your writing stronger and more engaging.

Clear out adjectives and adverbs. Descriptor words often serve to prop up weak nouns and verbs, like 'very sad' instead of 'heartbroken' and 'really old' instead of 'ancient'. Don't try to remove every descriptive word from your writing; they do serve a purpose. However, make sure they add their full force to your work by paring them with strong nouns and verbs.

Read your essay out loud or copy and paste it into an online text to speech generator. Listening to your essay can help you identify awkward sentences and misspelled words that your spell-checker might not catch.

Check for plagiarism. You should not be plagiarizing in the first place, but sometimes we accidentally copy wording. Run your work through a plagiarism checker to ensure that all of the content is uniquely yours.

Workshop

Finding other people who can read and critique your writing will be invaluable to your growth as a writer. Ask for critiques from people who are also learning to write, or who know how to write. During a workshop session, refrain from arguing with them or trying to answer their criticism on the spot. Listen quietly, take notes, and decide whether or not to apply their suggestions later. Pay attention to problems with finding your thesis or following your argument. If other people don't think your essay's goal is clear, chances are it isn't. Any clarity you see is coming from your meta-knowledge of the essay. Get feedback on what you need to do to provide clarity and try to implement the suggestions.

Conform to the Format

As you prep your essay for submission, check with your instructor or publishing organization as to the required format for the essay. Some common forms are MLA, Chicago, and APA. Correctly formatting your essay is a good way to boost your grade. Items you should check for conformance to format are as follows:

1. Font
2. Page numbers
3. Quote format
4. Page Margins
5. Title Page (if required)
6. Spacing (single or double)
7. Citation format
8. Necessary headers

I cannot stress enough the importance of the editing process as you complete your essay. Purge your writing of misspelling, grammatical mishaps, and formatting mistakes, and ensure that your argument and your argument alone is the focus of your essay.

Now, print out or mail in your essay and give yourself a high five!

Argumentation is an art learned through practice. While books like this can give you a jump start and keep you from making beginner mistakes, only engaging in active spoken and written debate can serve to really improve you as an arguer. If your first few arguments don't go well, don't beat yourself up. Learn from your mistakes and try again the next time. Keep applying yourself to being the best that you can possibly be, and you will be debating with the best of them in no time.

The great secret of the world's debaters is the mysterious union between preference and logic. Many thinkers relied on logic alone and found themselves without followers. Those who left logic and relied entirely on their own charisma did themselves and those who believed them a disservice and are remembered with amusement and disdain. Someone in the middle of the two is the perfect argument that people seek to construct.

Reason soundly, reason kindly, and you too can master the ancient art of arguing a case.

Conclusion

Thank you for making it through to the end of *Argument Structure: Secrets of the World's Best Debaters*. Let's hope it was informative and able to provide you with all of the tools you need to achieve your goals, whatever they may be.

Now that you know how to structure your arguments, you are ready to take on all kinds of situations where you want to present and defend your beliefs, from school to the workplace to public forums.

Many people never learn how to argue effectively. This can damage their confidence and make them angry, confrontational, and finally irrational. You, however, have everything you need to enter a discussion with confidence and compelling logic. Hold your head high and remember that if your argument is strong and true, the criticism of the angry and ignorant doesn't matter.

Finally, if you found this book useful in any way, a review on Amazon is always appreciated!